In Case of Emergency

JACQUI BRAUMAN

2nd Edition
ISBN: 978-0994514608

DEDICATION

To my husband, who tolerates my dreams and puts up with my workaholism. It's all for you. You are my 'why'.

CONTENTS

ACKNOWLEDGMENTS

Thank you to Kathryn Harris, who put me onto Source Bottle, where I found Getrude Matshe. Getrude, having to be accountable to you to get this book done quickly, and all your tips and tricks about the industry have been instrumental in producing my first book. Thank you so much. Finally, to Alexis Neely in the USA who is doing very similar work in her jurisdiction that I am doing in mine; your ideas and inspiration are a driving force to me changing the focus of my practice.

OTHER BOOKS BY AUTHOR

Jacqui has also written:

Death and Social Media
Acres of Diamonds
Steps to Success for Women
Graduate the School of Hards Knocks

SARA

1 SARA

Sara is a single mother raising her four-year-old daughter Michelle and two-year-old boy Matthew. Although she was devastated that her relationship with the father of her children failed, she has really embraced being able to do things her own way. She gets to choose what her children eat, what they watch, when they sleep, and where they go to daycare.

On the other hand, she moved away from her own home town to live with her ex-husband. But since the relationship broke down, she has stayed in her new town instead of moving back close to her family. She doesn't have any of her own family to rely on if she is exhausted or unwell.

Michelle is very intelligent, and highly sensitive. Sara suspects that she may be slightly autistic, but has not pursued a diagnosis with a pediatrician. Michelle thrives on routine, but equally she becomes very distressed and anxious when something out of the ordinary happens.

Matthew is mummy's baby. Sara sought comfort in him as an infant when her relationship broke down. He likes cuddles with his mother and glows in her presence. He is bubbly and happy with almost everyone, but only for short periods. He needs his mother.

Sara's ex-husband is immersed in a new relationship and has just had a new baby. He is only seeing the children one day every second weekend, and is really only doing this at the prompting of Sara. He has not showed any interest in learning their routine, and he expresses impatience and frustration with Michelle's quirks.

Sara works as a payroll officer three days per week, from nine in the morning until three in the afternoon. .

It's an ordinary day, and Sara bundles the children into the car to get them to daycare in the morning. Matthew starts to cry as soon as they pull out of the driveway. Michelle explains that he has forgotten his latest comfort toy: a zebra-striped pillow pet. Sara sighs inwardly and lets Matthew know that the pillow pet will look after the house and will be waiting for him when he gets home. Matthew sniffles all the way to daycare, and then he is clingy when Sara tries to hand him over to his room coordinator. Sara kisses him goodbye and wishes she didn't have to leave him, but she also wishes that he didn't make her feel so guilty about leaving. Michelle, on the other hand, marches off without hesitation and tells Sara that she will see her this afternoon.

Later, after an ordinary day in the office, Michelle decides to do a half hour circuit at the Curves gym that she is a member of. It is right at three o'clock, and it won't hurt for the children to be picked up a little bit late. There are other children at daycare who are there for much longer than her two.

Feeling energized and like she's really treated herself, Sara is buoyant and looking forward to picking up Michelle and Matthew.

But as she takes off through an intersection when her light turns green, a large 4x4 utility vehicle slams into the front driver's side of Sara's car and drives over her the front of her car. It ran a red light.

Sara is dazed, and she is stuck in the car for hours as emergency crews try to cut her legs out of the crumpled front of her car. She has taken a hard hit, her neck has whiplash and she is in shock. Her purse and ID were all in the foot-well on the front passenger side, and are stuck in the mangled vehicle. The emergency crews are working to free her, more importantly, than looking for her ID.

After three hours, Sara is out of the car and is taken to hospital. Her legs have been crushed and her spine has been bruised. She is likely to fully recover, but there will be months of hospital visits and rehabilitation ahead of her.

When the emergency crew got Sara out of the car, they then recovered her purse and put it in with her on her way to hospital. Other than her driver's license, bank cards and loyalty cards, there is no other information on her about who her next of kin are and whether she has children or not. Sara's phone was crushed and couldn't be accessed without a pin number anyway, which Sara is in no state to provide even if the phone was working.

The daycare center is getting worried when Sara hasn't arrived to collect Michelle and Matthew by 5 o'clock. This is usually the latest that she would ever be. Matthew is whimpering and clingy with the caretakers, and Michelle is waiting patiently near the front hall. She cannot be engaged by any of the caretakers to play. The daycare center tries calling Sara, but her phone goes straight to voicemail. They contact her employer, but they confirm that she left at three o'clock as usual.

Sara's next of kin is her mother, so the daycare center tries calling her, even though they recognize that it is an interstate number. The phone rings and rings, and then goes to a message service, as Sara's parents are taking a caravan holiday for three weeks. Even if she answered the phone, it would be three hours before Sara's mother could drive to collect the children.

Although they know it's a last resort, the daycare center does have contact details for Michelle and Matthew's father. They call him. He is angry to have been contacted. He is angry at Sara's irresponsibility for not collecting the children. He is in no rush and says he will be able to arrive in an hour, and asks that they call him back if Sara arrives in the meantime.

Most of the daycare center staff leave for the day, and the manager stays behind with Michelle and Matthew. She feeds them a cold dinner just before their father arrives. He is abrupt with them and demands to know from the manager what he is supposed to do with them. Matthew looks at him tearfully, and Michelle looks at the floor, pulling on a hank of her hair. The manager suggests that he take them home and put them to bed.

It is a horrible night for both Michelle and Matthew, and for their father and his new family. He doesn't have adequate facilities for them, and Matthew is inconsolable because he wants his pillow pet — he really wants Sara.

Eventually the police track down Sara's next of kin and they ensure that the children are safely with their father. Their father learns that Sara is in the hospital and likely to stay there for months. He is unprepared and doesn't know his own children.

With only short visits to see his mother over the coming months, Matthew is regressing. He is constantly tearful and pretending to be a baby so his father's new partner will cuddle him like her own infant.

Michelle is showing more worrying signs. She has been found pounding her forehead against a wall, and she has torn a number of chunks out of her hair. She is not talking or engaging.

When Sara is finally released from hospital, she wants to spend as much time with her children as she can. She can see the effect that her absence has had, but she does not have income protection insurance so she has to go back to work within a week of coming out of hospital. The children's recovery is longer than her own.

If Sara had an In Case of Emergency card in her purse, and some close friends who had instructions in case she had such an accident, then they could have been contacted and stepped in to act in the place of their father.

Make sure you have some plans in place and have an emergency contact who can get to your children. Make sure you have a process by which your emergency contact can be contacted easily.

Don't delay. For your own free In Case of Emergency card, go to www.incaseofemergency.net.au NOW.

PAUL AND AMANDA

2 PAUL AND AMANDA

Paul and Amanda have been married for fifteen years. They love each other deeply and are very comfortable in the routine that they have built for themselves. They have two children, Timothy and Tamara, who are ten and eight. Paul and Amanda both work, and their weekends are filled with sporting activities for their children. Paul plays golf on Saturday afternoons. Amanda likes to get out cycling early in the mornings. Timothy and Tamara are very active children, and are competitive with each other. Tamara is already as tall as Timothy, and is constantly trying to keep up with him and his friends in their cricket, basketball, skateboarding, or whatever else they are doing. Timothy is annoyed that his sister tags along all the time, but is protective of her should any of his friends have a go at her. Tamara has a few girlfriends, but she doesn't encourage them to come around on weekends or after school because she likes to roam around with the boys then.

Every September during school vacation, Paul and Amanda take Timothy and Tamara on a driving vacation. They pile into the car without solid plans, and they just stay in towns where they end up in and try to experience things spontaneously.

This September, Paul is driving them all up into the Blue Mountains, when they come around a blind corner and a large logging truck is coming the opposite direction, taking up the whole road. Paul swerves, but the road is narrow and the car careens down a cliff about twenty meters and stops suddenly against a large gum tree. Paul dies on impact. Amanda is knocked out. Timothy and Tamara are practically unharmed in the back of the vehicle.

Much too young to take responsibility, Timothy climbs out of the vehicle and clambers back up to the road. The truck didn't even notice what had happened, so it didn't stop. Timothy flags the next car that comes past, and they help to contact emergency crews to come and recover the car and Timothy's family.

Amanda has to be placed into an induced coma initially to help stabilize any potential brain injury. It was her wish that her dignity was paramount and that if she was unlikely to recover from such a condition, she be allowed to die. However, she did not document any of these wishes, and as Paul had already passed away, no one knew. She had not appointed a Medical Power of Attorney, so there was no one person to make medical decisions for Amanda. The medical staff consulted with Amanda's parents, but ultimately they just followed the recommendations of the medical staff because they didn't know otherwise.

Despite her injuries, Amanda is brought out of the coma within a few days. While recovering in the hospital, Amanda is grieving and trying to provide as much reassurance as she can to Timothy and Tamara. She knows that Paul didn't have a will, as they never got around to doing it.

Amanda contacts a solicitor for some initial legal advice, and is told that when someone dies without a will, they die intestate, and the State legislation determines how the estate is to be divided up. Amanda assumes that she will inherit everything of Paul's, because she and Paul were married. However, she is advised that the intestacy laws in Victoria specify that she will receive the first $100,000 of Paul's estate, plus all his personal possessions. Then she will only receive 1/3 of the balance of his estate, and the remaining 2/3 will be divided equally between her children. Timothy and Tamara will automatically inherit their portions once they reach the age of 18 years.

Because they had met later in life, Paul had already bought the house that was to become their family home when Paul and Amanda met. The house was in his sole name, although their mortgage was in both names. Most of their bank accounts were joint accounts, so they automatically transferred to Amanda's name, but Paul had a large savings account in his sole name, which forms part of the estate, along with the house.

Thankfully Paul had nominated Amanda as his sole beneficiary of his superannuation, so his death benefit paid out to Amanda directly instead of into his estate, and she was able to use these proceeds to pay the mortgage. However, since the estate is well over $100,000, Amanda is registered as a proprietor along with her children, and they are all listed as owners of the family home. She is unable to sell it and move on while they are minors without a court order, and once they are adults she will need their consent to sell.

Tamara, particularly, is effected by the loss of her father and when Amanda starts to date another man during Tamara's mid-teens, this pushes her over the edge. She believes that Amanda should stay faithful to Paul, and that Paul would be upset that Amanda is moving on with her life. She feels like Amanda is betraying her father. Her relationship with Amanda deteriorates dramatically, and they barely speak to each other for years.

Once Tamara turns eighteen, she knows she is entitled to her inheritance. She seeks legal advice and launches a VCAT proceeding to sell the house without her mother's consent because she wants the cash. Tamara is still living under the same roof with Amanda, and this adds an extra level of tension to the household and stress to Amanda's life. Timothy moves out during this time because he cannot stand the tension. Amanda's new relationship is also under significant strain. Amanda could buy Tamara out, but decides that she would like to sell and move on anyway, so the house is sold and Tamara receives her inheritance as an eighteen-year-old. Tamara decides not to go to university and moves in with some friends who don't work. They all live off Tamara's inheritance until it runs out and Tamara is left with nothing.

3 PAUL AND AMANDA - REVISITED

Paul and Amanda have been married for fifteen years. They love each other deeply, and are very comfortable in the routine that they have built for themselves. They have two children, Timothy and Tamara, who are ten and eight. Paul and Amanda both work, and their weekends are filled with sporting activities for their children. Paul plays golf on Saturday afternoons. Amanda likes to get out cycling early in the mornings. Timothy and Tamara are very active children, and are competitive with each other. Tamara is already as tall as Timothy, and is constantly trying to keep up with him and his friends in their cricket, basketball, skateboarding, or whatever else they are doing. Timothy is annoyed that his sister tags along all the time, but is protective of her should any of his friends have a go at her. Tamara has a few girlfriends, but she doesn't encourage them to come around on weekends or after school because she likes to roam around with the boys then.

Every September during school vacation, Paul and Amanda take Timothy and Tamara on a driving vacation. They pile into the car without solid plans, and they just stay in towns where they end up in and try to experience things spontaneously.

This September, Paul is driving them all up into the Blue Mountains, when they come around a blind corner and a large logging truck is coming the opposite direction, taking up the whole road. Paul swerves, but the road is narrow and the car careens down a cliff about twenty meters and stops suddenly against a large gum tree. Paul dies on impact. Amanda is knocked out. Timothy and Tamara are practically unharmed in the back of the vehicle.

Much too young to take responsibility, Timothy climbs out of the vehicle and clambers back up to the road. The truck didn't even notice what had happened, so it didn't stop. Timothy flags the next car that comes past, and they help to contact emergency crews to come and recover the car and Timothy's family.

Amanda has to be placed into an induced coma initially to help stabilize any potential brain injury. It was her wish that her dignity was paramount and that if she was unlikely to recover from such a condition, she be allowed to die. When she and Paul did their wills, they also appointed Medical Powers of Attorney and prepared Advanced Healthcare Directives. Amanda had selected that her Advanced Healthcare Directive was to apply if two independent doctors, one of whom needed to be a specialist, determined that she was unlikely to recover any independence. Amanda's treating doctors did not believe this was going to be the case, so the Advanced Healthcare Directive did not come into play.

Amanda had appointed Paul as her primary Medical Power of Attorney, but since he had already passed away, Amanda's alternative Attorney was her sister, not her parents. Her sister was a nurse and understood the medical treatment and terminology that was being discussed, and was able to make prompt decisions about Amanda's care, even when the medical team was recommending one form of treatment that was less risky than another. Amanda's sister was aware of the more risky treatment, and believed it to be more appropriate given Amanda's younger age and good general health. This treatment selected by Amanda's sister provided good results, and ultimately led to a quicker recovery by Amanda.

Despite her injuries, Amanda is brought out of the coma within a few days. While recovering in hospital, Amanda is grieving and trying to provide as much reassurance as she can to Timothy and Tamara. She contacts the solicitor with whom she and Paul had done their wills and other family estate planning. Her lawyer reassures her that the original will is safely stored in their strongroom, and that she doesn't need to do anything except forward Paul's death certificate onto the law firm once it arrives. They would get back in contact with her then.

Paul had nominated Amanda as the executor of the estate, along with the solicitor who had prepared the will. Since he owned their family home just in his name, he had left the house to her in a flexibility life interest, so she would be able to use the house and have the discretion to sell it to buy another house, or even sell it to use the proceeds for aged care, if required. The life interest ceased if she died or remarried. The balance of the residue of Paul's estate was left to Amanda outright. In the event that Amanda died or remarried, the house would then transfer equally to Timothy and Tamara, but was held in a minors trust until they reached the age of 25 years. Paul had also nominated Amanda as the beneficiary of his superannuation, so Amanda was able to use his death benefit to pay the mortgage off.

Tamara, particularly, is effected by the loss of her father. But when Paul and Amanda did their wills, their solicitor also offered to do a legacy video for them. This was a video that they did together, speaking about their childhood, their family, what they learned during their lives, what was important to them, and they also expressed their wishes for their spouse and children in the future. In the video, both Paul and Amanda said that they would want each other to be happy if the other died, and to continue living their life, and if that involved meeting a new person then that's what they each wanted. Amanda allowed Tamara and Timothy to watch this video whenever they felt like they needed too.

When Amanda starts to date another man during Tamara's mid-teens, Tamara is able to accept that this is what her father would have wanted, and doesn't feel like Amanda is being unfaithful to his memory. Her relationship with Amanda was not great during her teenage years, but after Tamara had lived independently for a couple of years, she and Amanda start to build a new relationship as adults.

Tamara and Timothy continued to watch the video of Paul and Amanda in their legacy video, to remember their father and his voice. They each gained important messages from the legacy that Paul had left behind, and each time they watched the video as they got older, they learned something else about their father and his life.

Amanda eventually decides to remarry. She understands that she will relinquish her life interest, so the family home that she shared with Paul will be transferred to Timothy and Tamara. Timothy has just reached twenty-six and Tamara will be twenty-five in just over a year's time. Amanda decides that it is best that the house is sold, and she will hold half the proceeds in trust for Tamara until she reaches the age of twenty-five, rather than renting the house from them. She consults both children, and the solicitor who is a co-executor, and everyone agrees with this course of action.

Amanda remarries and lives with her new

husband in his property. The old family home is sold, and Timothy inherits his half. Amanda invests the other half for twelve months, until Tamara reaches the age of twenty-five when she inherits it. Tamara has returned to university as an adult student and has formed a promising, stable relationship. She uses part of the inheritance for a deposit on a unit in her own name, and she invests the rest.

BONUS - Advanced Healthcare Directive

Please note, this document records your wishes and is not binding. There may be binding forms in your State, so check with your local solicitor.

THEOBALD LAWYERS

Advance Healthcare Directive

General

TO MY FAMILY, MY PHYSICIAN AND ALL OTHER PERSONS CONCERNED, THIS DIRECTIVE is made after careful consideration by me:

____

of ____

at a time when I am rational and of sound mind.

STIPULATION/S:

This Advance Healthcare Directive applies only if the following stipulation/s are met:

☐ If at any time I have become unable to participate effectively in decisions about my medical care.

☐ If two independent doctors (at least one a specialist) are of the opinion that I am unlikely to recover from a severe illness to a state of independence and competence, or that such recovery could only be to a state of profound physical or psychological suffering. Such an illness could include severe and lasting brain injury or dementia.

(Tick and initial the stipulation you want to apply. The condition that you DON'T want to apply, strike through the entire paragraph and initial at the end)

IF THE STIPULATION/S ARE MET, THEN IN THOSE CIRCUMSTANCES I DECLARE that I am not to be subjected to any medical intervention or treatment aimed at prolonging or sustaining my life, AND QUITE SPECIFICALLY:

(For each treatment, initial the column choice that reflects your wishes)

TREATMENT	I DON'T WANT	I WANT
Artificial feeding (nutrition and / or hydration)		
Antibiotics		
Artificial respiration		
Any surgical procedures		
Circulatory support including CPR		

TREATMENT	I DON'T WANT	I WANT
Corrections of abnormal levels of any toxic substance		
Blood transfusion		
Drug treatment of hi / lo blood sugar		
Drug treatment of hi / lo blood pressure		
Renal dialysis		

(Once you have initialled one of the choices for each treatment, draw a diagonal stroke through each of the unsigned choice boxes so that none if left unmarked).

AND, again where the stipulation/s apply, any persistent Distressing Symptoms are to be *maximally palliated* by appropriate analgesic, sedative or other palliative treatment, even though that palliative treatment may also have the additional consequence of shortening my life, AND QUITE SPECIFICALLY:

(For each Distressing Symptom, initial the column choice that reflects your wishes)

DISTRESSING SYMPTOM	MAXIMUM PALLIATION	NOT MAXIMUM PALLIATION
Pain		
Breathlessness		
Extreme weakness or Paralysis leading to total dependence		

DISTRESSING SYMPTOM	MAXIMUM PALLIATION	NOT MAXIMUM PALLIATION
Those caused by lack of food and fluid		
Psychological suffering such as fear, panic, terror, extreme anxiety or delirium.		
Loss of appetite, nausea, vomiting, diarrhoea or incontinence.		

(Once you have initialled one of the choices for each distressing symptom, draw a diagonal stroke through each of the unsigned choice boxes so that none if left unmarked).

AND, again where the stipulation/s apply, if it should be legal to do so at that time, I request that my death be hastened by a doctor providing or administering a fatal dose to allow me to die with dignity.

I wish it to be understood that I dread degeneration, prolonged dependence, inability to communicate and indignity far more than I fear death. I ask my medical attendants to bear this statement in mind when considering what my intentions would be in any uncertain situation. I hereby absolve my medical attendants from any civil liability arising from compliance with this Advance Healthcare Directive.

I RESERVE the right to revoke this Advance Healthcare Directive at any time, but unless I do so it should be taken to represent my continuing directions.

SIGNED BY ME: ______________________

this ________ day of ________________ 20

in the presence of:

____
Witness Signature

____
Witness Name

____
Witness Address

Attachment A: Your Health Status at Time of Signing

At the time of signing this document

(tick and initial the one that applies)	(initial)
☐ I am in good health	
☐ I have been advised that I am suffering from: ______________________________ ______________________________	

Attachment B: Your Medical Practitioner to Sign Here

I, ______________________________

of ______________________________

attest that ______________________________, is of sound mind.

______________________________ ______________________________

Medical Practitioner's Signature Date

Attachment C: Your Chosen Appointed Agent

(tick and initial the one that applies)	(initial)
☐ I have completed an Enduring Power of Attorney (Medical Treatment) form and appointed the following person as my agent: ______________________________ of ______________________________	
☐ I have not completed an Enduring Power of Attorney (Medical Treatment) form and have not appointed anyone as my agent.	

Attachment D: Organ Donation

In the event of my death

(tick and initial the one that applies)	(initial)
☐ I want to donate my organs for transplantation	
☐ I do **not** want to donate my organs for transplantation	

NICOLE AND MICHAEL

4 NICOLE AND MICHAEL

Nicole and Michael have both separated from their former spouses and have gotten together. Nicole has been separated from her husband for four years. They couldn't have children, which put the strain on the marriage which caused its ultimate failure. Michael has been separated from his wife for two and a half years. He and his wife have a fifteen-year-old son called James who lives with his mother, and he only sees Michael very rarely.

Two years ago, Nicole has moved into the house that Michael owns. The house was the investment property that he had bought with his wife while they were married. He transferred the former family home to his ex-wife and she transferred the investment property to him. They did all this by agreement, but they wanted to avoid legal fees so they didn't have any formal documentation done at the time. The house that Nicole and Michael live in has a mortgage in Michael's sole name.

Nicole works in the local library, and Michael has worked for himself as a sub-contractor for most of his life. He is a qualified electrician, and has a work vehicle that is full of his tools of trade. They also have a fishing boat and enjoy getting away on weekends to Lake Eppalock or Echuca.

Michael has a "turn" while he's on a job. He goes to see a doctor after Nicole insists that he see someone, and he finds out that he has some partial blockages in the arteries to his heart. He is scheduled for some minor surgery in a few months' time, and is given mediation and a strict diet and exercise regime in the meantime. This gives him a scare and he decides to see a financial planner associated with the bank he banks with.

Michael has not been paying himself any superannuation, so he is given advice about setting up a self-funded retirement account by his financial planner, and is also sold what he thinks is life insurance. Nicole is relieved that he has done something. Michael has never made a will in his life, and Nicole also suggests that he should see a solicitor to prepare one.

Unfortunately Michael never gets around to making a will. He has a sudden heart attack two weeks later and dies within hours.

Intestacy laws of Victoria will apply to Michael's estate, since he died without a will. Nicole is entitled to seek to administer the estate as Michael's current spouse, but she needs to provide sufficient evidence to the Supreme Court that she is his spouse. This is difficult to do, as they have not combined any bank accounts and all the house bills are in Michael's sole name. She needs to get friends to sign affidavits as to their knowledge of the relationship between her and Michael to prove their relationship.

Michael would have wanted Nicole to be able to live in the house — he wouldn't have wanted her to be on the street or having to relocate and rent. But he would have also wanted to make some provision for James. Unfortunately he didn't get any legal advice, and no one knows what he would have done.

None of Michael's potential wishes matter anyway. The laws of intestacy apply, so the spouse of the deceased gets the chattels (household contents and motor vehicle) and the first $100,000 of the estate. The remainder is then divided up between the spouse and the child of the deceased. The first 1/3 to the spouse, and the remaining 2/3 equally to the children.

Because Michael and his ex-wife never documented their property settlement after their separation, his ex-wife is still considered a spouse and is entitled to a claim of the estate. The ex-wife decides to make such a claim, so of the first $100,000 and next 1/3 of the estate, the ex-wife is entitled to 2/3 of that, and Nicole is only entitled to 1/3 of the spouse entitlement.

James will inherit the rest of the estate once he is 18 years old.

Once she is granted Letters of Administration to be able to administer Michael's estate, Nicole contacts the bank about Michael's life insurance policy. She is informed that it wasn't life insurance but accident insurance and, because Michael didn't die in an accident, there's nothing to pay. Without the payment from that policy, the estate only includes Michael's bank accounts which total about $14,000, his vehicle and boat, and the house. The house is valued at $320,000 and the mortgage is $280,000. So the value of the estate is only about $70,000. James will inherit nothing, as the estate is not over $100,000. Nicole is only entitled to 1/3 because Michael's ex-wife has claimed her spouse entitlement. So Nicole will receive about $20,000 after funeral expenses and legal fees are paid.

Nicole sells the house since she can't afford to refinance it and also pay out Michael's ex-wife. She has a garage sale to try to sell some of the more valuable possessions, but most of it is not worth anything so most of it is given to the Salvation Army. The proceeds from the sale of the house are only about $32,000 after the real estate agent's commission.

Nicole closes the bank accounts and sells the vehicle and the boat. She is exhausted and has been distraught throughout the whole process. It has taken nearly 12 months of her life, and in the end she inherits only $13,500.

She does hand over a box of photos and fishing trophies to James when Michael's ex-wife brings him to collect her cheque for her inheritance.

James is bitter at Nicole, because in his view she stole his inheritance. If she hadn't been in his father's life, his whole estate would have gone to James because his mother wouldn't have made a claim against it. James is bitter at his father, because in his mind his father was a loser, having left so little behind after his death.

James promptly throws out all his father's photos and fishing trophies. He remains bitter about his father for most of his teens and twenties until he has his own children. Only then is he able to reflect on how his father must have felt over the failed marriage. Even though he has been able to develop some empathy for his father, he still condemns his father as a poor provider and loser.

5 NICOLE AND MICHAEL - REVISITED

Nicole and Michael have both separated from their former spouses and have gotten together. Nicole has been separated from her husband for four years. They couldn't have children, which put the strain on the marriage which caused its ultimate failure. Michael has been separated from his wife for two and a half years. He and his wife have a fifteen-year-old son called James who lives with his mother and only sees Michael very rarely.

Nicole has moved into the house that Michael owns two years ago. The house was the investment property that he had bought with his wife while they were married. He transferred the former family home to his ex-wife, and she transferred the investment property to him. They did all this by agreement, but they wanted to avoid legal fees so they didn't have any formal documentation done at the time. The house that Nicole and Michael live in has a mortgage in Michael's sole name.

Nicole works in the local library, and Michael has worked for himself as a sub-contractor for most of his life. He is a qualified electrician, and has a work vehicle that is full of his tools of trade. They also have a fishing boat and enjoy getting away on weekends to Lake Eppalock or Echuca.

Michael has a "turn" while he's on a job. He goes to see a doctor after Nicole insists that he see someone, and finds out that he has some partial blockages in the arteries to his heart. He is scheduled for some minor surgery in a few months' time, and is given mediation and a strict diet and exercise regime in the meantime. This gives him a scare and he decides to see a financial planner associated with the bank he banks with.

Michael has not been paying himself any superannuation, so he is given advice about setting up a self-funded retirement account by his financial planner, and he is also sold what he thinks is life insurance. Nicole is relieved that his has done something. Michael made a will with his ex-wife soon after James was born, so Nicole also suggests that he should see a solicitor to prepare a new one.

Unfortunately Michael never gets around to making a new will. He has a sudden heart attack two weeks later and dies within hours.

Michael would have wanted Nicole to be able to live in the house — he wouldn't have wanted her to be on the street or having to relocate and rent. But he would have also wanted to make some provision for James. Unfortunately he didn't get any legal advice, and no one knows what he would have done.

Michael's old will appointed his now ex-wife as his executor, and left his whole estate to her. In the event that his ex-wife had already died, Michael left everything to James once he reached 21 years of age. The will is still valid, and since Michael and his ex-wife had not formalized a divorce, all provisions for her in the will are also still valid.

Nicole is sent a copy of the will, but is not kept informed about the progress of the estate. She is eventually sent a copy of the Grant of Probate that Michael's ex-wife receives to administer the estate, and she is also sent an inventory of what is included in the estate.

She learns that the life insurance that

Michael thought he had was not paid by the insurance company, because it was a policy for accident insurance, and was not life insurance at all.

According to the inventory, the estate only includes Michael's bank accounts which total about $14,000, his vehicle and boat, and the house. The house is valued at $320,000 and the mortgage is $280,000. So the value of the estate is only about $70,000.

The solicitors acting for Michael's ex-wife require Nicole to vacate the property, as the estate is selling it. Michael's ex-wife attends and has a screaming match with Nicole about what household items belonged to Michael and should stay for her to sell, and what Nicole actually owned. It is all too much for Nicole, and she is still grieving too much to argue over some of the items that Michael had given her.

With no place to live and all of Michael's inheritance going to his ex-wife, Nicole finally decides to seek some legal advice for herself. She is advised that she could make a family provision claim; as the current spouse she would be entitled to part of the estate. She cannot be given a definite estimate about how much she would be entitled to, or her chance of success. The estate is small and she is reluctant to incur legal fees, which she is advised will be paid by the estate. But she knows that Michael would have wanted her to have been provided for — he just didn't do a good job of looking after his affairs. So she decides to proceed with the claim.

Four months later, and a total of $20,000 of legal fees out of the estate, the estate is depleted to $50,000 and Nicole settles the proceedings for half of that. Her claim never gets before a judge — it is filtered through the legal system and pushed off to a compulsory privately paid mediation where two lawyers and two barristers and a mediator are well paid. She is given advice and is basically told that the estate is too small for her to take the matter all the way to trial, so she needs to settle it today. She is told that Michael's ex-wife also knows that she has to settle today, so Nicole doesn't have much leverage to negotiate what she would consider a successful outcome. She wanted the entire estate, as she believed would have been Michael's intention.

James is bitter at Nicole, because in his view she stole his inheritance. If she hadn't been in his father's life, his whole estate would have gone to his mother and then eventually to him, as his mother would have passed it on. James is bitter at his father, because in his mind his father was a loser, having left so little behind after his death.

James promptly destroys all the photos that exist of Michael. He remains bitter about his father for most of his teens and twenties until he has his own children. Only then is he able to reflect on how his father must have felt over the failed marriage. Even though he has been able to develop some empathy for his father, he still condemns his father as a poor provider and loser.

Moral: make sure your will is up to date — an out-of-date will can be worse than no will, so make sure your solicitor gives you advice about what to do for your children from a former marriage, and make sure you have life insurance left directly to your spouse or children.

CHECKLIST FOR YOUR PLANNING

❑ Choose executors — more than one, and at least one should not also be the guardian for your children. You should also consider a backup executor if something happens to your first choice

❑ Choose guardians for your children. These don't have to be family members. You should also have a backup guardian if something happens to your first choice. Also, if you want a couple to be the guardians of your children, consider whether you're happy for one of those guardians to continue caring for your children if one dies or they divorce

❑ Are there specific heirlooms or special items that you want to gift specifically to your children, or anyone else?

❑ Is it appropriate to leave everything to your spouse, or do you need to leave something directly to your children or create a trust for your children?

❑ What age do you want your children to be before they can control their inheritance?

❑ If you create a trust for your children, or they are under age to inherit, remember that your executor will control the money in the meantime. Make sure your executor has instructions about how you want them to invest that money and what you would allow them to use the money for until your child inherits it.

❑ If any of your children also die, or die before they are old enough to receive their inheritance, what do you want to happen to their share?

❑ Who is the beneficiary of your superannuation? Your superannuation does not automatically form part of your estate. Make sure you receive advice about the tax consequences of your beneficiary appointment.

❑ Are you excluding anyone from your Will that might have a claim? Make sure you receive adequate advice about this, or your estate may be wasted in legal fees.

❑ Have you finalized a divorce and property settlement with your ex-spouse, to ensure that no claim against your will can be made?

❑ Receive advice about what assets and liabilities are actually included in your estate, since jointly owned property is generally excluded.

☐ Do you need a Mutual Will Agreement with your spouse? Seek advice about this.

☐ Is there anyone you want to exclude from being able to be a guardian of your children? There are ways of leaving confidential instructions and evidence to prevent this from happening.

☐ Consider your need for Powers of Attorney, in the event that you have an accident, for someone to make financial and medical decisions on your behalf.

☐ Get advice about Capital Gains Tax consequences of transferring, retaining or selling some assets.

☐ Get advice about the impact of your will on someone's social security benefits.

SANDRA AND ASHLEY

6 SANDRA AND ASHLEY

Sandra and Ashley feel that they are the luckiest people alive to have found each other. They had both been divorced from their previous marriages. Sandra has two children, Rachel and Rebecca, and Ashley has three children, Jacob, Jett and Julia. It's a huge, crazy family, but it all seems to work. The house is full of laughter and affection.

The children are all in primary school, so mornings getting them ready are a whirlwind. Rebecca and Julia are the same age and in the same class — they are best friends and are inseparable. This is how Sandra and Ashley met, when the girls were in Prep together. Jacob is the eldest and is preparing to go to high school next year. Rachel is in grade 5 and Jett is in grade 4.

After school, Jacob takes responsibility for

all of the children to walk home together. Sandra gets home from work as a dental assistant by 4 p.m., and they have various sport training, swimming training and music lessons every day of the week. Ashley gets home from working in the branch at their local bank by 6 p.m., and they all eat dinner together.

One Thursday, Sandra is walking to her car on her way home from work. Something that has been lurking in her brain for years suddenly explodes — she has a brain aneurysm and collapses in the car park. She is quickly rushed to hospital, but nothing can be done. She dies.

When Sandra and Ashley married, they made wills together and made sure that they were each other's beneficiary of their superannuation account and death benefit. Sandra and Ashley appointed each other as executor, and left everything to each other, as so many other married couples do. They also appoint each other as primary guardian of their children, so that their former spouses don't automatically become the sole parent and guardian. Only in the event that they both passed away would any of their estate pass onto their children, and they had agreed to divide their combined estate five ways to their children equally.

Within 6 months of Sandra's death, her estate is finalized and Ashley has received everything — her bank accounts, her superannuation, the house that they were living in, and sufficient money from the death benefit to pay off the mortgage. He has been well provided for, and as guardian of Sandra's children, Rachel and Rebecca continue to live with him and the other kids. Because they've had that stability, while they miss their mother, they continue to be very high-functioning and happy children.

Six years later, when all the children are teenagers and less demanding of his time, Ashley meets someone new. They take it slowly, because Ashley puts the children first, but within 12 months Cathy has moved into the house with all of them. Cathy's children are both in their early twenties, and are living independently. Another 12 months later, Ashley and Cathy marry.

Ashley knows from having been divorced and remarried before that marriage invalidates a will. So he and Cathy attend a solicitor's office and have new wills done. While Ashley is generally very good at putting the children (now mostly young adults) first, he doesn't think of them in this context, and he isn't given proper guidance by the solicitor. Their wills appoint each other as executors and leave their entire estates to each other in the first instance. Only in the case that both of them pass away do the children get a mention, and then the combined estate is split seven ways, equally between their seven children.

Tragically, Ashley has a heart attack and dies within 12 months. The five original children are all over 18 years of age, though the youngest three still live at home in the house that was originally Sandra's.

They all attend the funeral on a Thursday one week after Ashley's death, and the following day Cathy moves out of the house. She becomes hard to get hold of, and she doesn't accept calls from Ashley's children.

Within two months of Ashley's death, a letter is sent by Cathy's solicitor to Ashley's children that they must vacate the house because Cathy will be selling it.

Unbeknownst to Ashley's children, although they suspect, Cathy has redone her will since Ashley has died, and appointed her two children as executors of her new will, and gifts her entire estate to her two children. Her estate will include Ashley's entire estate, as she is the sole beneficiary of his estate. Ashley's estate also includes Sandra's estate, which he failed to consider when he made his will leaving everything to Cathy. If not for Sandra's estate, Ashley would not have had a house without a mortgage.

Rachel, Rebecca, Jett, Jacob and Julia all seek legal advice together. They are strongly encouraged to make a claim against the will for their father failing to provide for them. This is particularly in the case of Rachel and Rebecca, Ashley's step-children, whose entire inheritance from their mother is now gifted to Cathy. They are advised that the area of family provision claims is a very uncertain one, so while it is likely that they will be awarded something, a proportion cannot be estimated. Although they are later told that if the provision to Cathy was based on intestacy (Ashley dying without a will), then Cathy would be entitled to about 1/3 of the estate and they would have to divide the rest amongt themselves. They are advised that the estate will pay their legal fees, so it won't cost them anything upfront. By lodging the claim they could also stall Cathy's sale of the house.

Another six months later, Ashley's children all attend a mediation with lawyers and Cathy and her lawyers. They are strongly advised to settle the matter at the mediation because the combined legal costs are already $50,000, which is taken off the top of the estate before anything is distributed. Their position is they at least want to retain the house. Ashley's superannuation and life insurance were paid directly to Cathy instead of forming part of the estate, but they argue that she has been well provided for by those payments. So while the house is more than 75% of Ashley's estate, that is what they want. Cathy agrees, after a full day of negotiations, but refuses to allow an additional amount for Ashley's children's legal costs to be paid. For the sake of having the matter over and done with, Ashley's children agree and realize that they will jointly have to raise the $50,000 from somewhere else — either by a loan or mortgage, or ultimately the sale of the house if they can't raise the money (thereby losing what they had aimed for in the first place).

Cathy goes off into the sunset, having pocketed over $700,000 of life insurance and death benefit money left to her by Ashley. Ashley's children are able to retain the house, though they have a joint mortgage of $50,000. Luckily they all get along well, as they all agree that the youngest girls, Rebecca and Julia, can stay living in the house for as long as they need too. All their inheritance is tied up in that house, so it is not capital that they have access too until the house can be sold. Rachel and Rebecca also have deep emotional ties to the house and may struggle to sell it in the future, which is something that they will all have to work out between themselves.

7 SANDRA AND ASHLEY - REVISITED

Sandra and Ashley feel that they are the luckiest people alive to have found each other. They had both been divorced from their previous marriages. Sandra has two children, Rachel and Rebecca, and Ashley has three children, Jacob, Jett and Julia. It's a huge, crazy family, but it all seems to work. The house is full of laughter and affection.

The children are all in primary school, so mornings getting them ready are a whirlwind. Rebecca and Julia are the same age and in the same class — they are best friends and are inseparable. This is how Sandra and Ashley met, when the girls were in Prep together. Jacob is the eldest and is preparing to go to high school next year. Rachel is in grade 5 and

Jett is in grade 4.

After school, Jacob takes responsibility for all of the children to walk home together. Sandra gets home from work as a dental assistant by 4 p.m., and they have various sport training, swimming training and music lessons every day of the week. Ashley gets home from working in the branch at their local bank by 6 p.m., and they all eat dinner together.

One Thursday, Sandra is walking to her car on her way home from work. Something that has been lurking in her brain for years suddenly explodes — she has a brain aneurysm and collapses in the car park. She is quickly rushed to the hospital, but nothing can be done. She dies.

When Sandra and Ashley married, they made wills together and went through the process of family wealth legacy planning. They each listed out all their assets and liabilities and worked out what they had to leave to each other to make sure that they were well provided for. Sandra and Ashley appointed each other as executor, along with one of each of their respective parents. They also appointed each other as primary guardian of their children, so that their former spouses don't automatically become the sole parent and guardian. They each decide that they don't have sufficient life insurance to provide for each other, so they take out a life insurance policy of $300,000 each and make each other the beneficiary of that policy. They then leave everything to each other, and in the event that both of them have died, they leave everything equally to their five children once their children reach the age of twenty-five years.

To make sure that if either of them died, leaving everything to the other, they wanted to make sure that their children still ultimately got a share of the estate. Should one of them remarry, they didn't want the entire estate going to the new spouse. They are advised that they could enter into a mutual will agreement with each other, which is a contract that would prevent them from changing their will should the other die, thereby ensuring that nothing will change and everything will still all go to the children.

Within 6 months of Sandra's death, her estate is finalized and Ashley has received everything — her bank accounts, her superannuation, the house that they were living in and sufficient money from the death benefit to pay off the mortgage. He has been well provided for, and as guardian of Sandra's children, Rachel and Rebecca continue to live with him and the other kids. Because they've had that stability, while they miss their mother, they continue to be very high-functioning and happy children.

When they did their wills, Sandra and Ashley also prepared a legacy interview video, where they talked about various things such as what it was like when they were growing up, where their family comes from, what they've learned and what they would like their children to learn from them, and some of their values. Rachel and Rebecca have this video to watch of their mother, to see her animated and hear her voice, and as they get older they take a lot of the messages from it.

Six years later, when all the children are teenagers and less demanding of his time, Ashley meets someone new. They take it slowly, because Ashley puts the children first, but within 12 months Cathy has moved into the house with all of them. Cathy's children are both in their early twenties, and are living independently. Another 12 months later, Ashley and Cathy marry.

Ashley knows from having been divorced and remarried before that marriage invalidates a will. But he also knows that he signed a mutual will agreement. So he and Cathy attend a solicitor's office and have new wills done. Ashley reaffirms his previous will, with one difference. He leaves 50% of his superannuation to Cathy, and the other 50% to be split between his five children. He then makes a binding nomination with his superannuation fund that his benefits are all to be paid to his Legal Personal Representative (the estate) if he dies.

Tragically, Ashley has a heart attack and dies within 12 months. The five original children are all over 18 years of age, though the youngest three still live at home in the house that was originally Sandra's.

They all attend the funeral on a Thursday one week after Ashley's death, and the following day Cathy moves out of the house. She becomes hard to get hold of, and doesn't accept calls from Ashley's children.

Cathy gets 50% of Ashley's superannuation and the benefit of another life insurance policy that Ashley had taken out and nominated her as the beneficiary directly. She goes off into the sunset and isn't heard of again by Ashley's children.

The children aren't twenty-five yet, so Ashley's estate is held in trust by their grandfather, Ashley's father, who is the executor of his will. There is a power built into the will that allows Ashley's father to release parts of the income or capital from the invested estate to use for the education or advancement of the children. The three girls want to go to university, so their inheritance can be used to help with some of the fees. As each of them reach twenty-five, their portion is released to them personally.

Jett marries in his early twenties and they divorce by the time he is 30 years old. He inherited about $300,000 when he turned twenty-five. He and his wife used this to buy a house. Now the house is included as part of the joint property of the relationship, despite Jett's major contribution, and his wife is entitled to at least 40%. Hence, a large portion of Jett's inheritance is paid to his ex-wife after the sale of the house that he bought with it.

8 SANDRA AND ASHLEY – REVISITED AGAIN

Sandra and Ashley feel that they are the luckiest people alive to have found each other. They had both been divorced from their previous marriages. Sandra has two children, Rachel and Rebecca, and Ashley has three children, Jacob, Jett and Julia. It's a huge, crazy family, but it all seems to work. The house is full of laughter and affection.

The children are all in primary school, so mornings getting them ready are a whirlwind. Rebecca and Julia are the same age and in the same class — they are best friends and are inseparable. This is how Sandra and Ashley met, when the girls were in Prep together. Jacob is the eldest and is preparing to go to high school next year. Rachel is in grade 5 and

Jett is in grade 4.

After school, Jacob takes responsibility for all of the children to walk home together. Sandra gets home from work as a dental assistant by 4 p.m., and they have various sport training, swimming training and music lessons every day of the week. Ashley gets home from working in the branch at their local bank by 6 p.m., and they all eat dinner together.

One Thursday, Sandra is walking to her car on her way home from work. Something that has been lurking in her brain for years suddenly explodes — she has a brain aneurysm and collapses in the car park. She is quickly rushed to hospital, but nothing can be done. She dies.

When Sandra and Ashley married, they made wills together and went through the process of family wealth legacy planning. They each listed out all their assets and liabilities and worked out what they had to leave to each other to make sure that they were well provided for. They then determined that their children should receive the benefit of any residue, which could be either held in trust until they reached the age of twenty-five years (a mature sensible age), or have a family trust set up in their will as a testamentary discretionary trust. Sandra and Ashley appointed each other as executor, along with one of each of their respective parents. They also appointed each other as primary guardian of their children, so that their former spouses don't automatically become the sole parent and guardian. They each decide that they don't have sufficient life insurance to provide for each other, so they take out a life insurance policy of $300,000 each and make each other the beneficiary of that policy.

At the time of making their wills, they had detailed advice and which trust to set up for their children — either a minors trust until their children reached twenty-five, or a testamentary discretionary trust.

The advantages of the testamentary trust were that it can provide asset protection if a beneficiary finds himself in financial difficulties such as bankruptcy, or if they are involved in a property settlement because of a relationship breakdown. The best aspect of a testamentary trust is the income splitting that can occur even to minor beneficiaries. In other forms of trusts, minors are taxed at penalty rates if income is distributed to them, but with a testamentary trust minors are taxed at ordinary marginal tax rates so that they can take advantage of the tax-free threshold (it can be useful for parents to have tax-free income to be able to pay for children's expenses). The disadvantages are the extra annual costs of an additional tax return each year, and other professional assistance that might be needed by the trustee, but this short-term cost can be outweighed by the other tax advantage within as little as 12 months.

Given the advice they received, Sandra and Ashley choose to put their entire residuary estate into a testamentary discretionary trust for their children.

Within 6 months of Sandra's death, her estate is finalized. Ashley has received Sandra's life insurance of $300,000 and the balance of the superannuation after paying off the mortgage on the house which Sandra directed was to happen. The house that they were living in, and all Sandra's other bank accounts and employee benefits, are transferred into the testamentary discretionary trust set up for Rachel and Rebecca. Ashley and Sandra's father are trustees of that trust. Ashley is also the guardian for Rachel and Rebecca, and Rebecca continues to live with him and the other kids. Because they've had that stability, while they miss their mother, they continue to be very high-functioning and happy children.

When they did their wills, Sandra and Ashley also prepared a legacy interview video, where they talked about various things such as what it was like when they were growing up, where their family comes from, what they've learned and what they would like their children to learn from them, and some of their values. Rachel and Rebecca have this video to watch of their mother, to see her animated and hear her voice, and as they get older they take a lot of the messages from it.

The investments in the testamentary discretionary trust earn enough income for Ashley to withdraw about $10,000 tax free for the benefit of Rachel and Rebecca each year. This supplements his income, which he has to use to keep all five children going, and makes it easier for him to cover some extra special things for the girls.

Six years later, when all the children are teenagers and less demanding of his time, Ashley meets someone new. They take it slowly, because Ashley puts the children first, but within 12 months Cathy has moved into the house with all of them. Cathy's children are both in their early twenties, and are living independently. Another 12 months later, Ashley and Cathy marry.

Ashley knows from having been divorced and remarried before that marriage invalidates a will. So he and Cathy attend a solicitor's office and have new wills done. Ashley also remembers the advice he received last time about the testamentary trust. The trust that was set up in Sandra's will has been a huge benefit for him, Rachel and Rebecca, and he wants to make sure the same benefits and protections are available for his children. Ashley's will appoints Cathy and his father as executor. He leaves 50% of his superannuation to Cathy, and the other 50% to be split between his five children. The balance of his estate in trust for his children, though excluding Rachel and Rebecca, who are his step-children. He then makes a binding nomination with his superannuation fund that his benefits are all to be paid to his Legal Personal Representative (the estate) if his dies.

Tragically, Ashley has a heart attack and dies within 12 months. The five original children are all over 18 years of age, though the youngest three still live at home in the house that was originally Sandra's.

They all attend the funeral on a Thursday one week after Ashley's death, and the following day Cathy moves out of the house. She becomes hard to get hold of, and doesn't accept calls from Ashley's children.

Rachel and Rebecca still aren't twenty-five years old, so they cannot become trustees of their trust yet, but their grandfather is still a trustee and is able to continue managing the investments for them. The trust also includes Sandra's house where they are living. They are entitled to 1/5 each of the 50% of Ashley's superannuation, so they direct that money into the trust as well, because they could see the financial benefit.

Ashley's other three children, Jett, Jacob and Julia, take their portion of the superannuation directly, but the balance of Ashley's estate, including his life insurance, all form part of the testamentary discretionary trust set up for them in Ashley's will.

Cathy gets 50% of Ashley's superannuation and the benefit of another life insurance policy that Ashley had taken out and nominated her as the beneficiary directly. She goes off into the sunset and isn't heard of again by Ashley's children.

As Rachel, Rebecca, Jett, Jacob and Julia get older, they all take advantage of the testamentary discretionary trusts set up for them by their parents, and reflect that they are grateful that their parents had the foresight and advice to set these structures up. They each split their trusts into individual trusts, as they are each old enough to become trustees of their own trust, but they still have their siblings as joint trustees as well. This is just as well for Jett, who marries in his early twenties and they divorce by the time he is 30 years old. There were mechanisms built into his trust such that he was not deemed to be in control of the assets and therefore they weren't considered part of the matrimonial property and his inheritance was safe from his ex-wife.

Each of them go on to have their own children, and they can utilize trust income for their own children too, so Sandra and Ashley's grandchildren are benefitting from their legacy. Each of them are able to draw tax-free income for their own children from the trust, increasing their disposable incomes and saving on paying tax. This extra money helps with bringing up their children with things that they would not have otherwise been able to afford, and taking advantage of opportunities that they wouldn't have otherwise had.

SAMPLE MUTUAL WILL AGREEMENT

This agreement dated the ____ day of _______ 20xx

Between

[Name and address] ("he")

And

[Name and address] ("she")

Whereby it is agreed by he and she that:

1. In consideration of the undertaking the obligations on his part set out in this contract, she will:
    1. execute forthwith a Will in the form set out in Schedule 1, and
    2. do all things necessary in order to ensure that the property in her estate devolves in the manner provided by her Will unless, and to the extent that, he or his legal personal representative consents in writing to her acting otherwise.
2. In consideration of she undertaking the obligations on her part set out in this contract, he will:
    1. execute forthwith a Will in the form set out in Schedule 2, and
    2. do all things necessary in order to

ensure that the property in his estate devolves in the manner provided by his Will unless, and to the extent that, she or her legal personal representative consents in writing to him acting otherwise.

3. The parties shall ensure that the copies of their executed Wills shall be annexed to each part of this Contract.

4. That parties shall execute this Wills in the forms set out in Schedule 1 and 2 hereof pursuant to the terms of this Contract, and agree that they will not at any time, during or after the lifetime of the other party, alter or revoke, or diminish the dispositions in, the said Wills without the prior knowledge and consent in writing of the other party or by an order of a Court of competent jurisdiction, save for any dispositions to the other party which are rendered ineffective by the death of the other party.

5. Each of the parties agrees that they will not do, or omit to do, anything with the intention of diminishing their estate.

6. This Contract applies to all assets owned by the parties at the date of this Contract, in addition to all assets subsequently acquired by either party during the concurrent lifetime of both parties. However, this Contract does not apply to assets acquired by the survivor of the parties after the death of the other of them, with the exception of assets acquired

or derived from the other party's estate.

7. This Contract is made with the intention that the said Wills shall not be affected or altered or avoided by any subsequent divorce or marriage of both or either of the parties within the meaning of the Wills Act 1997 or any successor to that Act, and that the said Wills may not be altered or revoked or the dispositions therein diminished without the prior knowledge and consent in writing of the other party or by an order of the court of competent jurisdiction.

8. This Contract is intended to bind the parties and/or their respective legal assigns during their life, and their respective executors or administrators following their death.

9. The parties further agree that this Contract shall not be varied or diminished other than by a formal deed of variation made between the parties hereto, or by an order of a court of competent jurisdiction.

10. Reference to "he", "him", or "his" is irrespective of gender and shall mean the applicable entity whether male or female.

Signed as an Agreement

Signed by ____ in the)
presence of:)

Signed by ____ in the)
presence of:)

DANIEL AND JENNIFER

9 DANIEL AND JENNIFER

Daniel and Jennifer were high school sweethearts who met again in their mid-twenties and never stopped their romance. They married within 12 months of meeting again, and worked on their careers for a few years, also buying a house. Jennifer is a nurse and Daniel works for a software development company but has an idea to develop his own mobile phone application. In their early-thirties, they have two boys within 18 months of each other, Callum and Cameron.

The next few years continue in a whirlwind and Callum and Cameron are soon in primary school. Daniel did develop his own mobile application, and made a substantial sum from that, which they invested. Additional income continues to trickle in from continued app sales, and they use this income for treats and toys for themselves and their boys.

The family does almost everything together. Jennifer limits her shifts to a few during the week, so that she can either do the school drop off or pick up. Daniel can do a lot of his work from home, so he works flexible hours and is able to help with the boys when Jennifer is working. They spend every weekend together, either with the boys' grandparents, or getting outdoors and visiting various places within driving distance. They want their boys to have as broad an experience as possible, to try as many things as they can, and to appreciate diversity of cultures and places. They are planning a four-week trip overseas with the boys in the coming months, around South-East Asia and one week in Samoa.

Rarely do they do anything alone together without the boys, but a few weeks before their big trip overseas, Daniel books a romantic stay in the heart of the CBD for them both. He plans an expensive dinner out, and then books tickets to a theatre. His parents are able to take the boys for the weekend. They are both eager when they drop the boys off the Daniel's parents place before heading into the city for their adult weekend. But after dinner and on their way to the theatre, they are walking across the street at an intersection and a horrific accident happens. A lady runs a red light and plows straight through the pedestrians crossing the street. The driver was travelling at about 40km/hour, which is not excessively fast, but it does a lot of damage. Daniel and Jennifer took the brunt of the force, holding hands as they crossed the street. They both died within days of the accident.

The driver was not drunk, but it didn't matter. She was charged with dangerous driving occasioning death, manslaughter and other back-up charges. No penalty could bring Daniel and Jennifer back, though.

Despite Daniel and Jennifer loving each other and their boys deeply, they failed to do any planning for their future in the event that such an accident happened. They had never prepared a will, had not appointed guardians for their children, and had not thought about life insurance or other structures that could make the future easier for their spouse and children.

Without wills, they had not appointed guardians. Daniel's parents had the boys when Daniel and Jennifer died and kept them with them until the funeral. At the funeral, Jennifer's parents tried to discuss future plans for the boys with Daniel's parents. Daniel's parents refused to make any commitments and refused to bring the boys around to Jennifer's parents for a visit. As the months passed by, Jennifer's parents were desperate to see Callum and Cameron, but Daniel's parents continued to refuse — Daniel's parents had always secretly thought that Jennifer came from a poor family and they didn't want to associate with her except that their son married her. This was now their chance to bring the boys up how they wanted to, and they decided to refuse any access to Jennifer's family. At wit's end, Jennifer's parents seek advice from a family lawyer and decide to seek Parenting Orders so that they can have access to Callum and Cameron, and so that the boys can spend some overnight time with them.

The family law proceedings for Parenting Orders are bitter, and Daniel's parents raise many unfounded objections and allegations about Jennifer's parents. This resulted in long affidavits filled with tit-for-tat attacks on each other, and large legal fees. Jennifer's parents are granted some interim orders for the boys to spend time with them during the day once a fortnight. When they attend, they are miserable. The boys are aware of the legal proceedings and miss their parents dearly.

They want to see Jennifer's parents — their Pop and Ma — but they have been made to feel guilty, like they are doing something wrong. They withdraw into themselves, away from both sets of their grandparents, and will only talk openly to each other. The family court orders a psychologist to do a report on Callum and Cameron, and the report is damning on the situation, and suggests that Callum and Cameron need significant psych report to try to undo the guilt and grief they are feeling. The legal battle goes on, as neither Daniel's parents or Jennifer's parents will accept the recommendations.

All of Daniel and Jennifer's assets were jointly owned. Their superannuation appointed each other as the beneficiary, but they did not appoint alternative beneficiaries. Because they died intestate, their estate is subject to the relevant State legislation. Because Jennifer was the younger of the two, she is deemed to have died second. All the jointly held assets are transferred to her name and form part of her estate. Her superannuation fund decides to pay her fund and death benefit into her estate. Because Daniel does not have anything in his estate, and because his superannuation company becomes aware of the legal battle for the children, they require a superannuation proceeds trust to be established for the boys before they will release any funds. As there are no appointed guardians of the children, and no legal personal representative for Daniel's estate, the superannuation company either wants the respective grandparents to all be trustees by agreement, or they insist that the public trustee will have to be the trustee of the trust. Of course, the grandparents cannot come to any agreement, so the State Trustees set up the superannuation proceeds trust to receive the funds, and they administer the investment until Callum and Cameron are 18 years old.

Under intestacy laws, Jennifer's estate will go equally to Cameron and Callum. They will inherit their share of the estate once they are 18 years old. Jennifer's parents apply for Letters of Administration to administer the estate on behalf of the boys. The Supreme Court asks further questions about the guardianship arrangement for the children, since the guardian for a minor beneficiary would usually be the one to make the application, so Jennifer's parents have to go through the process of detailing the battle in the family court for the Parenting Orders and that guardianship is currently in dispute.

Luckily, they are granted administration. The estate comprises of the house, the substantial investments from Daniel's mobile app, and other bank account and employment benefits that are paid out.

Callum and Cameron grow more and more sullen as they get older. They are bitter with their family, they hate themselves, they no longer speak to each other, and they have become fairly withdrawn from mainstream society. Callum, the elder of the two, starts associating with anti-social groups in his mid-teens and starts binge drinking and using recreational drugs. Cameron goes the other way and becomes a recluse, and lives almost exclusively online. They are unable to form any bonds with their family or grandparents at all.

At the age of eighteen, Callum inherits his half of the superannuation, and his half of the estate that has been managed well by Jennifer's parents. It is a substantial amount for an eighteen-year-old boy. He ends up attracting a group of people leaching off his money, and using drugs. He overdoses and dies by the age of twenty-two.

Cameron inherits the remainder of the estate when he turns eighteen. He buys himself a house and invests the balance, and lives as a recluse though his online avatars rather than engaging with the world. He doesn't need to work a traditional job. His online activities bring him some income, and his investments bring him the rest. He orders his clothes and food online and they are all delivered to the house. He has no reason to leave the house, and is very unwell physically and psychologically. He does not live the life that his parents would have wanted for him.

10 DANIEL AND JENNIFER - REVISITED

Daniel and Jennifer were high school sweethearts who met again in their mid-twenties and never stopped their romance. They married within 12 months of meeting again, and worked on their careers for a few years, also buying a house. Jennifer is a nurse and Daniel works for a software development company but has an idea to develop his own mobile phone application. In their early-thirties, they have two boys within 18 months of each other, Callum and Cameron.

The next few years continue in a whirlwind and Callum and Cameron are soon in primary school. Daniel did develop his own mobile application, and they made a substantial sum from that which they invested. Additional income continues to trickle in from continued app sales, and they use this income for treats and toys for themselves and their boys.

The family does almost everything together. Jennifer limits her shifts to a few during the week, so that she can either do the school drop off or pick up. Daniel can do a lot of his work from home, so he works flexible hours and is able to help with the boys when Jennifer is working. They spend every weekend together, either with the boys' grandparents, or getting outdoors and visiting various places within driving distance. They want their boys to have as broad an experience as possible, to try as many things as they can, and to appreciate diversity of cultures and places. They are planning a four-week trip overseas with the boys in the coming months, around South-East Asia and one week in Samoa.

Rarely do they do anything alone together without the boys, but a few weeks before their big trip overseas, Daniel books a romantic stay in the heart of the CBD for them both. He plans an expensive dinner out, and then books tickets to a theatre. His parents are able to take the boys for the weekend. They are both eager when they drop the boys off the Daniel's parents place before heading into the city for their adult weekend. But after dinner and on their way to the theatre, they are walking across the street at an intersection and a horrific accident happens. A lady runs a red light and plows straight through the pedestrians crossing the street. The driver was travelling at about 40km/hour, which is not excessively fast, but it does a lot of damage. Daniel and Jennifer took the brunt of the force, holding hands as they crossed the street. They both died within days of the accident.

The driver was not drunk, but it didn't matter. She was charged with dangerous driving occasioning death, manslaughter and other back-up charges. No penalty could bring Daniel and Jennifer back, though.

Daniel and Jennifer had been given free Will Kits when they took out life insurance over the phone with one of the insurance companies advertising on TV. They had followed the instructions and completed the wills pretty well — they were signed and witnessed properly, so they were valid.

They had appointed each other as executors, and their respective siblings as alternative executors in the event that they both died — Jennifer's sister Jane, and Daniel's sister Dianne. They both appointed

Jennifer's sister Jane as the guardian for their children in the event that they both died. They left everything to each other in the first instance, and they left their entire estates to Callum and Cameron if they both died, once Callum and Cameron reached the age of twenty-one years.

All of Daniel and Jennifer's assets were jointly owned. Their superannuation appointed each other as the beneficiary, but they did not appoint alternative beneficiaries. Because Jennifer was the younger of the two, she was deemed to have died second. All the jointly held assets are transferred to her name and form part of her estate. Her superannuation fund decides to pay her fund and death benefit into her estate. Because Daniel does not have anything in his estate, they require a superannuation proceeds trust to be established for the boys before they will release any funds. As the appointed guardian for the boys, Jane is required to set up the trust and be the trustee until the boys reach the age of eighteen years. Because the superannuation doesn't form part of Daniel's estate, there is no requirement for it to be held in trust until the boys reach twenty-one in accordance with his will.

Jane takes the boys into her care. She has

two children of her own, and lives with her husband in a normal suburban house. He parents come to see them a couple of times each week, and Jane often takes the boys to see Daniel's parents for a Saturday lunch. She also makes sure she invites them to any school awards and sports days.

Jennifer's entire estate is transferred to Jane to be managed until the boys reach twenty-one, and she also manages the superannuation proceeds trust.

Jane decides to use the proceeds from the estate to buy her and her husband a bigger house. She is certain that Jennifer wouldn't have wanted her boys to be sharing a room with her children, so they move into a large five-bedroom house. Because the boys are orphans, she also wants to make sure that they have a nice holiday every year. She uses the proceeds from the estate to pay for a holiday for all of them to northern Queensland or Western Australia every year. She doesn't want them to feel like they're missing out, so she gives them $50 per week pocket money, and they are generally given a fairly light reign discipline-wise. Jane and her husband believe that children need to make their own mistakes, rather than being given boundaries.

Jane is well-meaning, but Jennifer and Daniel certainly would not have meant for the boys' inheritance to have been used in the way that Jane has. They wanted their boys to respect money and grow up knowing how to save. They also wanted the boys to have well-defined boundaries, to have a curfew, and to put school work before anything else. Jane didn't know any of this.

Callum inherits his portion of Daniel's superannuation at eighteen. He buys himself a brand new car straight away, and lives life up at clubs for a while. Because of his partying, he doesn't do very well in his final year of high school and doesn't get a university placement. He decides to buy himself a carpet-cleaning business, which he pays too much for and then doesn't seek appropriate advice about how to pay himself, pay tax and market the business. The business goes broke within 12 months, and he is pursued by creditors. He loses his part of the superannuation inheritance to creditors of the failed business. Because there is no gift over clause in the Will Kit wills that Daniel and Jennifer prepared, Callum can call on his inheritance earlier, despite him not having reached the specified age of twenty-one.

Immature, he calls on his inheritance, and legally Jane cannot prevent him, so she hands over control to him. To avoid bankruptcy, Callum uses his inheritance to pay off all his debts, plus interest and legal fees of various creditors, along with his own legal fees. Callum is left with very little, and ends up working stacking shelves in Office Works.

Cameron has always been quieter and more careful. He inherits the rest of Daniel's superannuation when he reaches 18 years, but other than buying a new car himself, he puts the rest into his iSaver account. He does reasonably well in his final year at high school and gets into a computer science course at university. Instead of working to pay for his fees and books and other expenses, he continually dips into his iSaver account. He continues to live at home with Jane, so at least he doesn't have to pay rent. Cameron graduates from university about the same time as he turns twenty-one and inherits the rest of Jennifer's estate. One of his good friends in his computer science course has been on at him for years about them starting their own cloud software company. When Cameron inherits the rest of his money, his friend convinces him to back their new company. Cameron bankrolls the start-up, and most of his capital soon disappears in office rent, computer equipment and high wages that they are paying themselves. The capital is gone before they have produced any software, and they start the hard search for venture capitalists.

11 DANIEL AND JENNIFER - REVISITED AGAIN

Daniel and Jennifer were high school sweethearts who met again in their mid-twenties and never stopped their romance. They married within 12 months of meeting again, and worked on their careers for a few years, also buying a house. Jennifer is a nurse and Daniel works for a software development company but has an idea to develop his own mobile phone application. In their early-thirties, they have two boys within 18 months of each other, Callum and Cameron.

The next few years continue in a whirlwind and Callum and Cameron are soon in primary school. Daniel did develop his own mobile application, and made a substantial sum from that, which they invested. Additional income continues to trickle in from continued app sales, and they use this income for treats and toys for themselves and their boys.

The family does almost everything together. Jennifer limits her shifts to a few during the week, so that she can either do the school drop off or pick up. Daniel can do a lot of his work from home, so he works flexible hours and is able to help with the boys when Jennifer is working. They spend every weekend together, either with the boys' grandparents, or getting outdoors and visiting various places within driving distance. They want their boys to have as broad an experience as possible, to try as many things as they can, and to appreciate diversity of cultures and places. They are planning a four-week trip overseas with the boys in the coming months, around South-East Asia and one week in Samoa.

Rarely do they do anything alone together without the boys, but a few weeks before their big trip overseas, Daniel books a romantic stay in the heart of the CBD for them both. He plans an expensive dinner out, and then books tickets to a theatre. His parents are able to take the boys for the weekend. They are both eager when they drop the boys off the Daniel's parents place before heading into the city for their adult weekend. But after dinner and on their way to the theatre, they are walking across the street at an intersection and a horrific accident happens. A lady runs a red light and plows straight through the pedestrians crossing the street. The driver was travelling at about 40km/hour, which is not excessively fast, but it does a lot of damage. Daniel and Jennifer took the brunt of the force, holding hands as they crossed the street. They both died within days of the accident.

The driver was not drunk, but it didn't matter. She was charged with dangerous driving occasioning death, manslaughter and other back-up charges. No penalty could bring Daniel and Jennifer back, though.

Daniel and Jennifer had done comprehensive family wealth legacy planning with a solicitor a couple of years before. They had appointed Jennifer's sister Jane and Daniel's sister Dianne as joint executors. After going through a process of writing out all their parenting values, and then compiling instructions to the guardian for their children, they determined that none of their family members would bring their children up in the way they would want. They spoke to their best friends, Dane and Jemima, who were honored and accepted the appointment as guardians as soon as they were asked. Dane and Jemima have three children about the same age as Callum and Cameron. They promptly ask if Daniel and Jennifer would agree to be guardians for their children, and this is also agreed.

Daniel and Jennifer set up comprehensive testamentary discretionary trusts for Callum and Cameron in their wills, and specify that they cannot control or have a say in the administration to their trust until their reach twenty-five years. They also sign binding nominations with each of their superannuation funds that their accumulated money and their death benefit are to be paid to their legal personal representative, so that their superannuation will be guaranteed to form part of their estate should they die.

Because Jennifer was the younger of the two when she and Daniel were killed, she is deemed to have died second. All the jointly held assets are transferred to her name and form part of her estate. Her superannuation fund pays her money and the death benefit into her estate. Daniel's superannuation fund pays his balance and his death benefit into Jennifer's estate as well, as it formed part of his estate and he left everything to Jennifer in the first instance. Jennifer's entire estate, a substantial sum of over $1 million, is transferred to Dianne and Jane to administer. They seek financial advice and make a variety of diversified investments.

Dane and Jemima promptly step in when they learn of the accident, and take the boys from the care of Daniel's parents who had them for the weekend that Daniel and Jennifer were killed. Callum and Cameron have spent lots of time with Dane and Jemima, particularly after the families grew closer when they discussed the issue of guardianship for their respective children. All the children know each other very well, and they create a loving and protective family around Callum and Cameron to support them through their grief.

Daniel and Jennifer had left comprehensive instructions to their guardians about things that were important to them in their own lives that they wanted their children to share, as well as parenting values on discipline, education, extra-curricular activities, sport and financial education. Their values closely reflect those of Dane and Jemima, so it is not hard for them to follow these instructions. But importantly, due to Daniel's interest in computer programming, he wants both boys to participate in extra education in that area, or at least be given the opportunity. Jennifer also felt particularly strongly about the boys being good swimmers, and to be involved in water sports, so Dane and Jemima embrace this too and involve the whole family in these sports.

The trust that Daniel and Jennifer set up included provision to be made to the guardians to help with the financial upbringing of Callum and Cameron, so with Dianne and Jane's joint approval, income is often released to Dane and Jemima to help with extra activities and expenses for Callum and Cameron. Dane and Jemima are not left out of pocket by bringing up Daniel and Jennifer's boys. In fact, their whole family is richer for it in many ways, and Callum and Cameron exceed in school and social aspects of their lives.

Callum does well in his final year of school. He gets into sports science at university, and because he is eighteen years old, he deals directly with Dianne and Jane to have income released from the trust to him for university fees and books. Only expenses that Dianne and Jane approve jointly are paid for, so when Callum asks for them to buy him a new car, they let him down lightly and suggest that if he works and saves $5,000 then they will match that amount for him to buy something second hand. He does achieve this, and goes onto finish his degree with honors. He takes over control of his trust when he turns twenty-five years of age, and is mature enough to seek financial advice to continue investments. When he marries, he buys a house in the trust, instead of in his own name, and continues to reinvest income from the trust to grow his wealth. When he has children, to help pay for extra expenses, he is able to draw income from the trust in the name of his children (Daniel and Jennifer's grandchildren), tax free up to $18,000 per annum (under the current adult marginal tax threshold). This significantly helps with the expense of raising children, and he is able to fund private school education for them.

Cameron also does very well in his final year at school, and gets into a double degree of commerce and computer science, following in his father's shoes. One of his good friends in his computer science course has been on at him for years about them starting their own cloud software company. When Cameron comes into the control of his trust at twenty-five, after a few years of working hard for other people, he and his friend decide to start their own business. Cameron seeks financial advice, and decides that his trust can loan the new company some capital to start-up. A commercial loan arrangement is entered into, so that the new company will be required to repay it to his trust along with interest at 7%. Both Cameron and his friend continue to work in their regular jobs as they grow their company on the side, until it replaces their income and they can work on growing it full time.

PREPARE FOR YOUR PLANNING – SELF AUDIT

DEPENDANT(S) – SPOUSE AND CHILDREN			
RELATIONSHIP	**NAME**	**SEX**	**DOB**

OTHER PERSONS WHO MAY BE INTERESTED IN YOUR ESTATE	
NAME	**RELATIONSHIP**

THE IMMEDIATE FAMILY TREE

PARENTS AND IN-LAWS

SIBLINGS AND THEIR SPOUSE AND CHILDREN

ASSETS

Asset Type	Name of Asset	Identifying numbers	Owners names
Bank accounts			
Real Estate			
Bonds			

Shares			
Personal property			
Loans owed			
Business interest			

LIABILITIES

Liability type	Name of liability	Identifying numbers	Owners names
Mortgage 1			
Mortgage 2			
Mortgage 3			
Consumer debt			
Tax			

Guarantees			
Loans			
Credit cards			
Sureties			
Other			

LIST OF COLLECTABLES, OFFSHORE AND SUBSTANTIAL NON-INVESTMENT ASSETS

Description	**Location**	**Value**	**Date acquired**

ABOUT THE AUTHOR

Jacqui Brauman is the principal solicitor and director of Theobald Lawyers Pty Ltd t/a TBA Law (www.tbalaw.com.au). She has a Bachelor of Laws, Bachelor of Accounting, Advanced Diploma in Taxation Law, and a Masters in Applied Law (Wills and Estates). Jacqui also has an accredited specialisation issued to her by the Law Institute of Victoria in the area of Wills and Estates.

Practicing mainly in wills and estates, and property law, Jacqui's career of 10 years has taken her from Central Victoria to rural New South Wales, to Sydney, and back to the outskirts of Melbourne.

Jacqui's primary focus in her wills and estate practice is to make sure young families know the consequences of not undertaking proper planning, and ensuring that their children are adequately protected, both physically and financially. Her message is simple: In a world of uncertainty, we cannot live with our heads in the sand. Instead, we can make sure that we don't leave a difficult mess behind us if something should happen. Then, hopefully, the plan never has to be implemented. But it's better to plan for security than try to struggle during grief and loss.

Public school educated and raised in Wangaratta, Jacqui is married to Daniel Brauman, who is a serving member in the Royal Australian Army. Together they do plenty of adventurous sports, including motorcycling, kayaking, camping, 4x4 and fishing. Jacqui also enjoys distance running and yoga.

Made in the USA
Monee, IL
04 November 2026

67386985R00066